the Octopus
and other poems

the Octopus

and other poems

Jennica Harper

John Barton, Editor

Signature
EDITIONS

Cover design by Doowah Design.
Photo of Jennica Harper by Stephanie Co.

We acknowledge the support of The Canada Council for the Arts and the Manitoba Arts Council for our publishing program.

This book was printed on Ancient Forest Friendly paper.
Printed and bound in Canada by Marquis Book Printing.

Library and Archives Canada Cataloguing in Publication

Harper, Jennica, 1975-
        The octopus and other poems / Jennica Harper.

Poems.
ISBN 1-897109-10-5

        I. Title.

PS8565.A6421O38 2006   C811'.6   C2006-901263-6

Signature Editions P.O. Box 206, RPO Corydon, Winnipeg, Manitoba, R3M 3S7

for Mom

On August 20th and September 5th, 1977, two extraordinary spacecraft called *Voyager* were launched to the stars. After what promises to be a detailed and thoroughly dramatic exploration of the outer solar system from Jupiter to Uranus between 1979 and 1986, these space vehicles will slowly leave the solar systems— emissaries of Earth to the realm of the stars.

—From the preface to *Murmurs of Earth: The Voyager Interstellar Record* by Carl Sagan, F.D. Drake, Ann Druyan, Timothy Ferris, Jon Lomberg and Linda Salzman Sagan, 1978

Contents

Horizons

If Roberta Bondar Were My Mother _____ 10
Leia: A Star Wars Love Poem _____ 11
Breasts: Case Study _____ 12
Regeneration _____ 14
Dragonfly _____ 16
Vocabulary of a Bush Pilot's Wife _____ 18
Between Eleven and Five _____ 19
To La Tuque _____ 20
Favourite _____ 21
Correlated _____ 23
Of a Father-Daughter Relationship _____ 24
Screw Roses _____ 25
Horizon _____ 28

Maps

A View of Port Angeles _____ 30
Witness to Love _____ 32
First Paradox _____ 33
April, 1975 _____ 34
The Colours of John Dillinger's Death _____ 35
Las Vegas _____ 36
Mass Transit _____ 37
Witness to Fear _____ 38
Cinema Paradiso _____ 39
Useful _____ 40
Two Blows _____ 41
The Legacy of the Jazz Age _____ 43
Maps _____ 44
Travelogue _____ 45
Warm Front _____ 46
Sea Life _____ 47

Space Junk

Lost Men in the Year 2000 _____ 50
Symbols _____ 51
The Man from Wisconsin _____ 52
Late Bloomer _____ 53
Sunspots _____ 55
Standstill _____ 57
Space Junk _____ 58
Rocket Scientist _____ 59
Tether _____ 60
Visibility from Space _____ 61
Trajectory _____ 62

Known Space

The Octopus _____ 64

Aerial

Sunday Night After the Snowstorm _____ 78
Sentient _____ 79
Thirty Years Ago Today _____ 81
Road Movie _____ 83
Nights Above Fraser Street _____ 84
The Bid _____ 85
His Version _____ 87
Thinning _____ 89
Autumn Detail _____ 90
When You Clean the Aquarium _____ 91
Aerial _____ 92

Acknowledgements _____ 95

Horizons

If Roberta Bondar Were My Mother

Maybe I wouldn't sleepwalk.
I wouldn't launch forward,
arms out, groping
in darkness,
wouldn't care about
borders, edges, wouldn't be concerned
with my own limits.

Astronauts sleep
with their arms straight out,
somnambulistic,
as if blind, or reaching
to embrace a child.

Maybe if Roberta Bondar were my mother
I wouldn't have any desire
to see things fall from the sky:
dead stars, snowflakes,
vapour trails,
another city's rain.

If she'd held me in one hand,
like an egg blown out,
maybe I wouldn't care about anything
bigger than a teacup.

Leia: A Star Wars Love Poem

Help me, she said, you're my only hope. I was listening.
Her body, as well designed as a compact car, smooth tail,
well oiled, aerodynamic, great headlights. Help me,
she said, through dust-blue electrons, a body
appearing out of nothing, a memory-clip, a slip of a girl.

A girl I wanted;
wanted to be.

◆

I would follow her anywhere, chase her across
galaxies, trying to hold on to my cool. Her cool.
She could be enslaved again, chained up, could be
falling out of love and wanting someone to help her,
some fool   like   me.

Through shining-white hallways, across forests, on sand,
she's speeding attractively away.

◆

I'm wearing white. I don't look like her.
The robe doesn't fall right, my hair's covered
by a brown bun-wig. Counterfeit. I've stopped
looking. Who will believe this synthetic hair, these breasts
and hips straining beneath a sheet?

The stars aren't cooperating.
They sit there, dumb, refuse to streak.

Breasts: Case Study

Then

I don't remember a time when I touched them,
suckled, struggled.
My first glimpse at the body's memory—
how we forget.

In the shower
with my slender mother,
her shameless
shapes: the C-section scar,
a trimmed, sexless V,
and breasts like perfect water
droplets.

Mine

At ten, they were already plush
like something you'd win at the fair.
I wouldn't admit I needed a bra.
Wanted to wear undershirts,
like the popular girls
who were as flat as the boys,

the blobs on my
chest just extra weight,
jacket pockets filled
and turned inside out.

Shame
on the outside.

When I touched them
it meant nothing.
Like trying to tickle myself.
Or practicing a kiss
on the back of my hand—
just skin on skin.

Hers

My mother's breasts
continue to face forward.
They know the way.

Like a young boy
I want to know what they would do
under my hand—how much
pressure they could withstand
before they gave.

How they might reveal
what is true and false in a body.

Now

When I cup myself,
I see my hands moving
over my mother's still
ripe breasts, how they will
form their rounded double-
you, how the hand
will believe anything.

Regeneration

Twice every winter on bonfire nights
the neighbourhood burned chairs and desks
and even evidence, I imagined, but never
books. An accumulation of newsprint
and wood near the top of the fire
tumbled to the ground inevitably
in an avalanche of cinder and soot.
After bonfire nights, it was time
to start again

but winter never ended.
Always outside and frostbitten,
we stabbed trees with spigots;
the intravenous lines produced
a thin blood, sticky and harmless.
I poured the hot liquid on the snow
and waited for it to harden,
for it to be solid enough to eat.

I would rather not have been
outside at all. I'd rather have sat
on the brown shag rug plucking words out
of my word-box, a game designed
to teach me how letters go together,
how the words sound, but not how to say
when will we move away from here?

The world was covered in white.
I thought that even farms were like this.
That the half-size school bus chugging
up the hill to my door
every day was only
this, because no other place
existed. At night, my young mother
dreamed of a farm, the dust and grain,
the place in her anxious marrow.

I believe in this—that I was the persistent,
nagging vestige of another life, born
to remind her that there is *home*
and there is the place
in which one simply lives.

I studied stickers of sparrows on windows,
trying to read them like traffic signs
in bird language:
Not here, not here.

Dragonfly

A spot of cloud leaves us chilled
in its slow wake. To get to this lake we had to follow
a hidden gravel road, had to listen for the sounds
of children.

Dozens of dragonflies hum
around, alight on the picnic table
with mechanical clicks. Click buzz whirr
as if they had helicopter hearts,
wings of wire.

When I was a child of six, a praying mantis
landed on my small calf,
sent spiny shadows down to meet my own.
I willed the tiny robot
to take interest in something else, wanted
to hear the grind
of metal bones collapsing.

The air here smells like turtles.
Makes me know it's real here,
and that I am here, too.

The thin roads circle and square
all around us. Every turn reveals a new tableau—
black tarps over rows of ginseng
growing hot and moist; white bee-hives
like clusters of lighthouses mark
departures, returns.

If I have been dreaming and wake
to see the same lake, the trees
pregnant with themselves, the two
eleven-year-old girls on the square island of dock,
I might think I am home. I might not remember
the word for the smooth valley, its simple
up-and-down.

But at home the moment isn't real.
Where are the girls? The sounds
of dragonflies like a call to arms?

Vocabulary of a Bush Pilot's Wife

I forget there were times my mother loved him—
and that she wasn't reserved
about it, that she was open,

she wasn't frail. Every gesture
was performed with certainty:
the job abandoned, the tongue stuck out
in defiance. But now she can say it—

We were still very much in love,
and I know this is what let her sleep
nights in small-town Quebec,
no company during the days
but the gas stove, the dictionary, the half-
done tapestry of a woman

sitting by the window, her long hair
in a loose, thick braid.

Between Eleven and Five

in the morning, the upper channels
zig and zag, give birth to great divides
of neon, static, huge swatches of light,
jagged lines pulling at
women. A tug one way,
body parts warped and inconceivable,
all colours in reverse—

like an invisible hand
is grabbing your breast,
yanking it into strange
points and peaks,
or mammoth ovals
with their crooked nuclei.
The breast goes from one side of your body to the other,
pulsing to the beat:
thrum, bum, chickadum-pah.

Those are the hours you are indecipherable,
elusive, impossible to catch and pin
down, not just your body moving
in and out in time, but your face.
Like gasoline on a lake.

To La Tuque

Even before I was born, Dad
took her places in the car. Before all
the drives away from home,
before the marathon-missions
without hotels, listening to "Piano Man"
or "Horse With No Name"—

they drove the long stretch
from Toronto to La Tuque
in an old black Jaguar,
the chrome cat long gone.

She insisted on bringing the budgie.
He told her there were budgies in Quebec,
but she said they wouldn't understand her.

During the hours on the highway,
the signs evolving from English
into French, the budgie screeched
and puffed itself up, and my mother
kept the windows open.

She couldn't hear anything
above the suction. The wind on her face
made her feel like that absent
cat, its smooth body
lying in wait.

Favourite

Your mother is twenty-two, straight
brown hair to her shoulders, flimsy
as dust. The yearbook shows her left
of twelve teenagers cradling mute
guitars. She has taught them to sit, how
to hold their heads,
how to stand, arms and wrists
loose and ready. She was there when they
tuned the strings, when they
sang first words waveringly,
when they were afraid.

Your mother sits with you
on a piano bench. You are five;
you would rather be writing
words in the evening
air with a sparkler.
Your hands are small,
you are sure they can't make
the reach: you fumble
with your zipper,
let that rhythm out, *zag zag*.
She lets you off too easily.
You will not sit on that bench
for ten years.

Your mother is fifty-two. You own
a classical guitar with new
nylon strings, and a book.
You even have a favourite
chord; you play it again
but the guitar is out of tune.
You want to give up but

your mother, saying nothing, takes
her seat at the piano, strikes a high E
for you to match. You twist and tune.
She will go all night if she has to,
E, E, E. You can't
remember sitting so still.

Correlated

Russian nesting dolls know
more about their origins
than I do. I know who begat
my mother, and who begat hers,
and then it all gets fuzzy.

But the dolls go back a good
six generations—each daughter
resembling her mother, in yellow
babushka and purple shawl, but not
so much as to be exact duplicates.
How beautiful, this
simple math.

I know we will never have that family reunion:
divorce makes us mismatched—
misnomers. The women in my family all
unrelated, a grouping of exes who stay in touch,
keep their last names the same.

When you lay the lacquered dolls out
you don't get a family,
only one side of it divided,

the dolls made out of wood
from the side of the family tree
that keeps branching up and left,
left, left.

Of a Father-Daughter Relationship

a limp windsock, a
shed snakeskin

a two-pound trout
hanging from
the thinnest of threads

Screw Roses

Past walls spray-painted with names:
the letters look familiar,
but foreign.

Past poor kids in frayed parkas.
No one where they're supposed to be.

We march down Jarvis, resisting
the shivers. It's sure to be
cold this Hallowe'en.

The hole-in-the-wall tattoo parlour
is guarded by James, a cluster of bones
in a T-shirt. A black mane like a girl's.

He shows us roses, blades,
daggers wrapped in roses.
We're not mall girls, Liz says.

Cheryl wants something elaborate
around her skull, something her hair can cover.
He won't do heads or faces.

I like the 50s, or what I know
from TV: leather jackets and motorbikes.

I want to be a bad girl, hanging out
with the mean guys, loyal but unpredictable,
adored, adorned,
a leader of the pack
                    (*vroom, vroom*).

The others go first, submit
to the machine like a dentist's tool.

He takes a fresh needle

from its package, small and simple;
my face is set. I am ready
to be tagged.

ii.

No. This is not ink. It can't be.

I have drawn on my hands,
have doodled endless black knots
on my thigh.

Do you want to stop for a cigarette?
James asks. My desperation—I don't smoke!

This is not one
needle but one thousand

                    Think of the war:
                    soft, thin boys
                    volunteering

flaming needles
barbed needles

                    their hair falling
                    in a halo around them

needles penetrating my skin
like hell's sewing machine,

in and out, but never
really out

               your pride—
               dogtags in the mud—

can't get used to it

thinking about the pain
I hope to defuse it,

hope to stop crying, to

               Run-run-run-run-runaway.

       iii.

When it's over, we are quiet.

Outside, a Hindu family walks
in a line, their gold trims glinting.

Jack-o'-lanterns unlit on doorsteps.

Everything in deep focus.
The outlines of shadows on the ground
as sharp as wire.

I walk with a limp,
refuse to put my jacket on.

I'm different:
unkillable.

Here is my war wound,
here is my scar.

Now you will know me
when you see me.

Horizon

On the night I am first kissed
seriously, the Saskatchewan sky
purples.

I leave my body.

I can see him, a head taller,
pointing out a stringy shooting star,
a rogue blinking something. My hand
is a child's. He spreads it open

in both of his, runs his thumb
along the fine creases of it, invents
my future, tells me I am to be
kissed, and the moody sky
pulses above everything
happening below.

When the kiss comes
it is warm and tricky and I can't connect
its dots, can't form an image in my mind.
But I think of warm water in the middle
of all this hot dry land.

Maps

A View of Port Angeles

from Victoria's great wall,
the breakwater, at midnight:
five women walk a line. We follow
close and careful, single-file, like we
were taught during fire drills
in public school. Waves hurtle
themselves against the concrete
below, and we are
shy and small, and they
can't reach us.

A twelve-minute walk, like this. We time it.
At the end, we sit against the lighthouse
graffitied with the glamorous
rock letters K-I-S-S,
the S's like cartoon bolts of lightning pointing
down, as though we might not remember
what is there.

        Here, a man and a woman
in raincoats gather into each other, sorry
we have come. This, everything, strikes
us as funny. Red wine
is poured into paper cups
and we all drink—toast the pulsing
city lights across the water
in another country.

On the way back along the wall,
each of us pretends
to throw our body
down into the water
as it breaks. We all want it:
the freedom to be broken.
And one by one, each of us
smiles at the pretender and says

Please. Don't even. Step away
from the edge, you're scaring me.

Witness to Love

She is sure catastrophe
follows her:

the kid with a gun
in his pocket,

the mysterious envelope
on her doorstep,

the too-late
airbag.

When she tells him
she is sure she will die
in pieces,

he goes to her ear,
says *Come here*,
his hot breath corresponding

to the bomb exploding in her lap.

First Paradox

after the Challenger

Snowflakes still pinned
to the classroom's walls.
Ten-year-olds gather around a TV. It's lunchtime,
spring, they should all be outside
at the tetherball, or playing
four-square ferociously. But they watch the news
at noon, see replays of the explosion. It can't be real,
they decide, they wouldn't just let those people
die. There is a notion of what is fair.

But: the numbers. The word
unusual. Time minus zero—
breathless, airless, absolute.

The footage rewinds in her eye.
The replayed memory of an explosion should be clean,
like a line of paint down the road, marking
this way; that way. But in a child's memory,
there's a distance between *real*
and the collision of fire and light:

earlier, Halley's tiny white tumbleweed
in the eye of a telescope,
which she is almost sure
she saw.
        And earlier still,
the springtime solar eclipse, the sun and moon
bottled and brown
through a welder's mask.

April, 1975

Irving Layton
stands over my mother,
eyeing her belly, the skin and silk around me,
as though it were a portent of his death.

He has read to the class and prophesied
ends and beginnings,
the slaughter of language, a language of slaughter.
My mother has caught his eye:

Layton predicts I will be a boy,
creating a future for me that I cannot resist—

foretells my handwriting, the sloping weak scrawl
of a teenage boy, a careless boy,
      the almost-but-not-quite loops,
      the stabbed dots on the eyes.

The Colours of John Dillinger's Death

A knock. The door opens.

Ah no, not you again, with the microphone:
you have nothing better to do than bother
a poor Romanian lady? Can't you see, I'm just a mother,
a girl who did what I was told?
                              Yes, I delivered his bones.

(clears throat)

I know what they're saying, but
the dress was orange, not red, it was the light
in the movie house that made it look red;
and the doctors who came to examine the dead
say his eyes were brown. But I saw them that night,
they were grey. His hair was the colour of the earth. And his lips, his lips
  were roses

before we walked out of the movie house door
into the trap.
              Then his lips fell silently apart,
blue, bruised.
              Do I love this man who decomposes?

(a pause)

As I have said before, of course not. And I have done more
than my part. So please, tell them not to deport me, have a heart.

Click.

Las Vegas

Las Vegas is a ghost town. Everyone you meet, a ghost.
No newspapers anywhere.

A haunting jangle follows you in and out of rooms
filled with smoke stale like attic waste.

You can tour the world here, all on one street: see the sights
at one-third scale. We are in the middle of nothing

and everybody else is here, too. A group of little people,
six-foot twin black women, brides wandering with troupes

of bridesmaids, men in bermuda shorts double-taking. All of you
here expressly to spend money, as if it were a treat

to put it into machines, on tables, on trays, into buckets,
perhaps into panties or up noses. A town drowning in need,

a small town. A colourful pop-up book page in the desert
where the senses overtake all sense, until there's only a desire

to get out, now, before this place erases you.
                                        From the plane
we parallel the Grand Canyon. Vegas, man-built and lit

fades quickly, but the trench goes on for hours—shale shelves,
tinted and highlit by the sun, life-sized, full of only itself

and yet the ghosts come with you, sit beside you,
their dead eyes rendering the canyon down to half its size.

Mass Transit

after Keith Haring

Here is a list of what is seen: dog, pyramid, UFO, man,
woman, pregnant woman, penis, television,
birth, Mickey Mouse, man with hole through stomach,
muscles, dolphin, angel,
plus sign, bright baby (with and without angel wings),
three windows for eyes and
many many
squiggly lines.

        Here is a list of what is believed: dogs can jump
through the holes in men. People can fly. Birth is a cartoon and
sex is funny at least some of the time.
What is on TV is not as much fun
as what's surrounding it, that's you and me. The pyramids were made
by aliens in UFOs,
as was Mickey Mouse,
not by Egyptians or a white man who later owned amusement parks,
as is commonly held as true. Men can and do
live with holes in their middles
for at least a few years, enough time to write a memoir. Colour can hurt.
People are cruel but it is forgivable.
Art is for the young.
Art moves fast.

Dying is painted in different colours than living, and:
chalk is cheap.

Witness to Fear

Sometimes she has visions.

He thinks it is charming,
perhaps that she is imagining things,
or she is a medium for the dying,

any of which might be a little bit true.
In the moment, though,
what she sees is real:

a woman carrying a raccoon
like a handbag;

on the unmade bed,
the coiled viper;

a honeybee the size
of her own head.

When she lays them all out like cards,
she can see what it is that
keeps her flushed:

anything in extreme close-up,
anything bigger than her hand's grasp.

Cinema Paradiso

Only a true believer
sits on the edge of her seat at the movies
like they do *in* the movies.
I am such a believer.

I know a small theatre
that can't afford to heat the room
even while the show is on. The projectionist
bickers with his girlfriend, ignoring
the reel that occasionally
sticks to itself and blinks.

The seats here are lined up along thin
steps, irrigation strips
lit from the seams, covered
in a sticky film and stains.

I'm convinced that one of these times
while everyone else is busy not believing
the paisley in the carpet will open
up and swallow us whole.
I try not to look down.

A machine-insect with a head of chrome
gnashes and bleeds milk. All car parts and teeth,
but also a mother,
it clatters around like a spider.
Just as it descends on the heroine
for the penultimate time,

a phone faintly rings
behind me and to the right,
four, five, six times.
Ringing and no one is picking up,
no one is coming to save us, her, me.

Useful

For my fifth birthday, everyone gives me seeds:

a crown of flowers
to wear on my head;
four small rubies;
three Mexican
jumping beans.

The collection sits on my dresser,
almost out of reach. Below them,
tucked away, are the useful
things: underpants and socks,
denim jumpers, pajamas
with dancing cats,
penguins walking
under pink umbrellas.

The seeds stagnate
on my dresser—

the beans are tiny pets I want
to tame, console, ingest.
The rubies are missing a ring
and I place them in a circle.
But the crown of flowers, I
pull apart, splay all over the room,
slip into cracks in the floor's
slats, grow a new garden,
I let everyone know
how good I am at taking things apart,
at putting beautiful, alive
things on display.

Two Blows

On the kitchen counter,
a glass inside another glass.
Water in between, no
pulling the two apart. The puzzle
has been sitting like this
for over a month,
a problem to be solved, or,
in all probability,
disposed of.

Then, an impulse: hold
the glasses in the sink.
Take a knife, blunt end
down, and lean away
from the anticipated
trajectory. Shut eyes.
Break the inner glass.
It takes two blows.

Math was always the problem;
the reason why playing
pool seems so difficult.
Why it's easy to trip
up a step, or tap a foot
on the beat
in between.

The inside glass crackles,
sprays out in unexpected ways.
How did that chip make the angle
around and past the stove?
There are chunks and hunks
under the toaster, inside the kettle,
on top of the fridge.
No cuts, though.

And no understanding of lines, shapes, patterns, pi,
so no way to predict a thing.

Inside the intact glass, there is a second glass,
still formed, but now mosaic;
its partial shape remains
but will fall away the moment
it is touched. Like a heap of ashes
after the bomb—it'll happen so quick
it won't feel done until it's undone.

The Legacy of the Jazz Age

Surely the way this ceiling
curves in on only one side
and blends smoothly into the wall
instead of intersecting sharply
is not at all what the architect intended.
Surely he was pressured into squeezing
his idea into a smaller one, a man
asked to put less in his suitcase,
a child ignoring the rules about
where the tabs fit into the slots
properly. All the evidence is here.
No god would slap together five
or seven misshapen partitions
and expect to have a room,
unless commissioned to.
I want to know who was paid
to make such a strange box,
imperfect and taller than it is
wide, the window a well-
placed and oversized distraction
that fills the corners with sun
between three and five;
I would like to find that man,
hold him, thank him.

Maps

At thirteen, I know the capitals
of every American state,
and the states in alphabetical order:
Alabama, Alaska, then the two
that start with "Ar."
I can conjure the states with my eyes closed,
can see the sunny yellow of California,
the lilac of Louisiana.
                    For two summers
I follow my father around Florida, wait
in outer offices while he has impromptu meetings
somewhere deeper in the square buildings.
Every waiting room has a map, each one
with tacks on different cities.

At thirteen, the continent is a giant mermaid
with its Mexico tail,
its bare-pink Canada breasts,
the brass tacks a necklace
of underwater treasure, and on the maps
the arrows for ocean currents
are the signs for motion
that keep the mermaid swish-swishing
through the water on the wall.
Always just arrived
or just going.

Travelogue

You sit across the table, palms up; the coffee
cups are empty, but they never stay that way long.
I hear about the six months you've been gone—
in Taiwan, stoned and sunburned, you recklessly
rode your own motorcycle on dirt roads.
                                    I can just see
your half-forgotten ex-girlfriend, who's along
for the ride, clinging to you like a guitar strap. And in Hong
Kong, you stayed up all night, danced with a stranger: she
drove you home just as dawn woke.
                                    The movie of all this
is grainy 70s Scorsese, tones of red, of gold;
the music by Tom Waits, for your friend's
bar, Rain Dog, in Taipei.
                                    Why you'd come back to this wetness
I don't know—Toronto's winter is bleached, is bitterly cold—
but I want to know. Roads. Like the backs of your hands.

Warm Front

All the teenage girls with hair piled up,
cuffs rolled up, lips curled tough and wise,
have come out of iron doors rubbing their eyes.
They've been waiting for the rain to finally stop.
Now the sun has opened up the sky again
and the girls have taken back the day: everywhere
they are lying back on the grass, smooth legs bare,
shielding their eyes with a loose salute. When
I think of how I was then, I'm amazed—confident
moment to moment, my real face well concealed
by a haughtiness time has revealed
to be cowardice. I know now I'm transparent
to girls who live outside, are invulnerable to tides.
Who refuse to be only one place at a time.

Sea Life

She has never wanted to be a pirate, an oarsman,
a galley maid, a mate—

but at twenty-six she goes sailing.
A beefy thirty-footer
trailing a dinghy like a white duck.
He laughs at her careful steps
along the deck.
                But sitting on the bow
spread eagle, she feels like Slim Pickens
mastering the bronco, the bomb.

When she takes the dinghy
to shore—its graceless plastic,
varnished oars—she feels it:
both hands must be in sync,
must listen to each other, to the water,
the wind.
              She has no internal rhythm
but somehow, she rows steady.
He watches, body tethered to the boat,
his hand casual around a taut rope.

Up close, the shore explodes
with purple starfishes.
Miniature crabs with exaggerated abs
dance on the rock bed.
She turns the dinghy around,
pulls water, pushes air.

She sees her hand gripping the oar,
the tip in the water, the water teeming
with pale jellyfish, sucking
and pumping. The barnacles
sprung from rocks
crackle and spit when
she comes near.
Everything spitting and pumping
and opening
and closing,

she wants to get back to the boat,
back to him—but thinking
about the beat, she loses it, rows
in circles.

She glimpses him waving to her
with both hands now, and thinks
for crying out loud, grab hold of something.

Space Junk

Lost Men in the Year 2000

You are obsessed with rockets:
their mean glare in Florida mid-morning,
what they're made of, what they hold.
Where they're going. You are concerned
with flight of all kinds, long distances,
emergency landings, power.

I am interested in the same things: men
adrift, floating weightless and infinite,
their silverwhite shells
an echo for the round world.
Is lost not knowing
where you're going, or rather, knowing
you're going nowhere at all?

You are moving to Montreal.
I don't know where you'll be
on New Year's Eve when all
the machines die. I only hope
to see you somewhere between
the century's pale and parting surfaces.

Symbols

One giant loon,
black arms spread
to welcome us
to our first motel.

The largest nickel ever
burned, serrated
edges and all, gleaming
in sunset sun and casting
angular shadows.

A statue of one man,
running.

I have a photograph of you
under the Vegreville egg—
your egg, K, that colossal
Faberge ellipse. Both you
and it brown and yellow
in the surreal twilight.

Your pale arms are spread.

The picture's heart is full
of grain. It's as if you hold
a planet high above you,
reach out, become the boy
you were when you were
someone's child. But there
is nothing between your hands.

The Man from Wisconsin

Martha stands next to a man
from Wisconsin, an expert
on pussy willows.

He shows her each variety, a dozen
in all: black pussy, giant pussy.
This is how they're talking.

Each stalk, Martha lifts
tenderly, caresses daintily
with her calloused fingers.

Runs her fingertips
along the plump furry pads,
asks, where do they grow?

Are they related to
the weeping willow?
She remarks on their beauty,

on their smoothness.
Martha is in love, and not
with the man from Wisconsin.

She is lost in the idea
of something so perfect:
half plant, half pet.

Oh, Martha, who runs their calluses
along the stalks of you,
and do they, as they should,

with reverence
remark upon your many
textures?

Late Bloomer

At twenty-four I learn to dance:
my cousin, nine years older
and Maid of Honour, wearing purple
and tassels, leads me into the hot spot,
the middle of the dance floor.
It is her goal to teach me to follow.

Here, she says, *feel my legs
on either side of yours.
Keep your thigh touching mine.*

At the spa, she told me that "Buffalo"
means *loose*. Buffalo wings, in thin
sauce, falling apart
between your fingers.
Everywhere around us, women
were caked with thick mud.

She pushes into me,
her purple velvet crushing my fake
silver satin, stocking to stocking.
Suddenly *Buffalo gals won't
you come out tonight?*
means something different.

Who were those soldiers and sailors
who wanted the sure thing
in the back of a friend's Ford?
Didn't they know even the good girls
could be easily led?

I was one who couldn't wait
to be the third base some boy would get to.
     In a red car, at the edge of a cliff,
     I am a paper doll,
     the tabs are being slipped out
     of their slots, new ones put in.

She leads me
with sure steps and strong arms
holding me upright;
my steps back, side, back,
I'm trying to stay loose, to
not stand still.

Sunspots

After throwing up every day
for three weeks, I take the bus
to St. Paul's Hospital,
the place you were born.
Its bricks aged and red.
Catholicism, like a paint job,
hangs over everything.

Your mother came here
when she suspected you:
watched you appear on the screen,
a tiny light grown huge, a sudden
helicopter in the night sky.

On a table I am probed,
tummy covered in goo, panties so low
pubic hair is exposed. The technician
says "I don't see anything."

If I tilt my eyes right, imagine right,
I can see a beating, the place
where our baby might be.
But it's just scratches on a screen:
Hubble photos, just gases and sound.

I'm sent to another room,
follow the line of blue paint
down the hallway. When your mother
birthed you, did she create
that parallel line of red?
Was everything well labelled
except this new life in her lap? You,
a new element in the world, already
listening to the clack of heels
down the hall.

I drink barium, lie back, roll
around for the camera as it
captures what's coated and empty.
I have a waking dream
of your mother's long labour,
the doctors pulling you out
with salad tongs.

After, on the hospital lawn,
I throw up all the barium,
it comes out strangely smooth,
white paint splattering my shoes
and a parking meter. The white on grass—
I think of football fields and rules

and your mother, who'd
always imagined you in black and white,
just blips on a screen,
sunspots, words on a page,
her shock when you came out:
your hair, so red.

Standstill

On the way home from the aquarium
I fall asleep against the window—
dream lightly of the caimans
who lie underwater on the rock floor.

We're stopped in Friday evening
traffic, near the beach
where we tangled our legs. I wake with the heat
of the Amazon, my hairline wet,

smelling only gasoline and salt.
Now it is me who can't
remember where I am, who doesn't know what to say.
You want me to say something.

Our first afternoon sleep together,
you had talked without waking, had said
Soon, I will be blind. Later you told me
you were worried you'd say something
worse, that you'd give yourself away.

As this small car starts to go,
you tell me about the man on the radio
who's playing three saxophones at once.

Space Junk

Head down, you
listen to
a song, pulling out
the memorable riffs and
changes, as I sit on the edge
of the bed and watch you
wrench it apart, put it back together—

you stop, hear the wrong note,
point to the hole in the air where the music
took you out of itself, where you accuse it
of carelessness.

A gentle gravity separates us, always
has. My words to you carry on jetstreams,
circle up and around your head like bees.
I see them buzzing there,
bait shamelessly designed
to lure you away, but you are lost
to me. Words fall
into oceans all around us—

the force of sound
is heavy and weighs me down. I am hungry
for a kiss; I taste iron in my mouth,
the memory of blood.
I see in the movement of air
the falling debris
of intricate plans,
abandoned.

Rocket Scientist

It never seemed to me before
that your fingers, nibbled and tough
could be agents of grace.
I have for many years
seen a left hand measure out
predetermined equations
up and down the neck of a friend.
Just as long, I've seen
a right hand chopping with
a magically even temper.
The two go together—
left sets it up,
right doles it out:
cause and effect called music.
I pick up a guitar for myself,
questioning my inner balance,
and what's worse, I question my eyes
and ears and hands.
You make it look so easy.
I want you to see me
with a guitar, a partner
I hold by one shoulder and
under one arm
in waltz position;
I want to be seen and believed.

Tether

My brother protects me from
balls of fire. This is how he is—
a controller

of all flying objects.
He sits in a booth
above the terminal,
eyelashes dripping sweat,
watching the levels. The skyscapes
of higher, highest, the strips
of cirrus, cumulonimbus:
he keeps it all together in his head.

How did he get like this?

We would sit in the car
and watch the two-props take off.
And at the museum of flight,
we could not tear our eyes away
from the replica of Kittyhawk:
Orville's fine, slender hands.

Everyone needs somebody
to hold them
to the ground. My need
for flight is connected
to his mind, a white line
on a black screen, dots
and dashes alive
on the retina.

Visibility from Space

Your friend is speaking of the Three-Rivers
Dam in China, a sixty-five year
project now in Year Fifteen: "Sons
will be brought in as children,
will become men"—transporting blocks
like dead meteors to a centre,
then another centre,
and the centre will keep changing.

The dam will push up into the moist
sky for nearly a mile.
We construct analogies—how many
football fields, how many stories
of a skyscraper. The air
will be unbreathable.
And also: who thought of this?

Your friend stands to get us beer
from the cabin. Beach sand
goes with him.

When he comes back, we are quiet,
frightened of the numbers, of serious plans.
He says, "The same sons will grow old,
will retire during the build."
There is no explanation in this.

We think of the boys
who start as saplings,
then ossify
into pillars, only to bend
back down, looking
at the still
raw, immovable earth.

Trajectory

*In the day's first hours consciousness can own the world
like a hand enclosing a sun-warm stone.*
                              —Tomas Tranströmer

Cupped from a great distance,
the earth is smoother
than a billiard ball.

All terrain evened:
valleys filled,
mountains levelled
by relativity.

In the cradle of orbit
it spins and warms
its soft skin.

On the beach lies a woman
in a bikini, her taut
swelled belly revealed
between bits of lycra.

Known Space

The Octopus

Right now, *Voyager 1* and *2* are pushing deeper
into known space. They will, like so many great American
home runs, go far beyond the fence, across the street
and through a window. They will never be recovered.

In a laboratory in Pasadena, at tables cluttered
with cold cups of coffee and dot-matrix printouts,
men interpret what *Voyager* sees: the spotty volcanic
surface of Io, the irregular shape of Amalthea.

Voyager carries greetings
from Earth. Simple diagrams
of how our genes
spool. Of the body of a man. Of where
we can be found,
like the map in the mall:
We Are Here (note how
the third dot in line is given
more emphasis, stationed slightly above
the other eight).

Also presented are rows of numbers,
the elements of us:

hydrogen, carbon, nitrogen, oxygen
and phosphorus

the modest recipe of our shared life.

~

I wish the world's memories well.
I have my own secrets—shoeboxes
and albums full of scribblings,
tokens from misplaced
friends and lovers.
Everything I keep is paper,
already disintegrating.

But while I'm here
I'll think of you, imagine
you with your newest love
who looks so much like you.

      The two of you get steamed up like clamshells—
      half-moon arcs on the sea bed.
      When you are both concave
      you come together, disappear from view;
      when one is concave, one convex,
      you form a perfect circle.

    ⚮

It is amazing what thoughts
we let slip in and out like mosquitoes
through the window.

    ⚮

Along with the math of us, *Voyager* lugs
gold-plated albums etched with our essences:
photographs, sounds heard on earth—in nature
and on highways and in the womb. Greetings
in fifty-four languages, and enough music
for some all-night cosmic dance-a-thon.

∾

Our lives orbit discretely these days, seldom intersect.

Now we trade thoughts on paper—
long distance chess,
one move at a time.

You tell me you can't condone the reckless hope
of finding some other life out there.
Can't fathom the waste.

∾

But think, just think,
        what it says about us
that we are even looking.
        That we can build
symbols of ourselves,
        will willingly become
stick-figures
        in an effort to describe
ourselves to others.

That we can admit we're not the only subject
and can sometimes be the searcher, the verb.

        ⌣

We have always discussed what we believe.
You do this with truths, I do it with fictions.
For you, it is Bakunin, Connolly,
that curmudgeon Adorno,
everyone's forgotten great-uncle.
For me, it's Purdy and Nowlan
and others who liked to put it plain.

        ⌣

Well, think of it like this:

a man in a lab coat
is a man in uniform.

♨

How slow is slow? Our messages are out there,
are on their way, but they are taking so long that
the transmission of the television show you are
watching right now will pass them within the hour.

♨

What is it about a lack of love
that weakens us to love the next time?

Simple economics, supply and demand.
We desire what we do not have
and will do anything.

♨

You can't believe that Sagan and his cronies
really want to find new life. They're looking
for the *Star Trek* alien: the gorgeous woman
who is human, but with painted green skin.
They want to find life like us, with only small
differences—larger ears, a pronounced brow.
They want to be the gods of everywhere.

(So unfair!)

～

I hold that it is noble, in a crazy way, to dream
of someone on a galactic beach opening our package
like a birthday present. Who knows what they will
do with it, if they will understand the instructions
to play the records. If they will interpret
a photograph the way we do.

I admit that for me, it is always
a little girl on that beach. A child without a face
tearing at our boxes stuffed with records,
photos, junk.

～

You are studying the octopus: its alienness,
its total lack of likeness to our own bodies.
A cephalopod, or "head-foot"—its brain and nerves
go all the way through. It moves all parts
independently: the small brain delegating
movement, the tentacles themselves
deciding where to go. Democracy
at its finest.

The octopus can pour itself through
any hole larger than its eye.
Cousteau said they can
recognize some humans.
But we do not
recognize them.

⚬⚬

Our messages won't even have left our solar system for 20,000 years.

⚬⚬

We pay to know
that our memories are safe.

⚬⚬

The records will last one billion years.
There is so little erosion in space:
just cosmic rays, slow-moving dust.

Ours was quicker:
what was a joy
became a chore.

࿇

Imagine a small West African tribe watching a film for the first time. It is
a documentary film about them. After, they are asked what parts they
enjoyed most. Each member of the tribe mentions the same thing: the
moment when the chicken flew. There had been a shot in which a
chicken had accidentally flown through the frame. The tribe members
did not know what happened in the rest of the film, because their eyes are
unaccustomed to following such fast light. For them, the film is about a
chicken.

࿇

Carl Sagan conceived the *Voyager* missions.
When, on the street, he would be asked
about his search

     (turning to answer the anonymous soul
          like Houdini to his executioner,
               not a second to prepare)

he would say we sent them because
it is important to try.

But how could they change our world? you ask.

(In the unlikely event our objects are found,
the sun will have put itself out long ago.)

᭴

This has always been our way—
a chair is never just a chair.
Love is never just love.

I wonder what things meant
to you, how my actions and words
were organized into a basic
theory of me.

᭴

Will we find anything?
I think it's gonna be a long, long time.

It is hard to imagine a thing in space.
In photos, *Vostok I* is a glass bauble,
a flammable beehive. Yuri spent
his 108 minutes of fame there,
not much more than
a glint in the eye.

Buran, for the Russian "snowstorm,"
was launched once, and is now
a restaurant.

> *Mir*, like the termination of an idea
> tested and failed, love cooled,
> falling back to earth so
> predictably.

᭜

Objects don't float through the universe like desire. They are both push-
ing and pulled as they follow possible trails, trace invisible spines in the
dark.

᭜

Voyager is a spy
sent to find new enemies.

᭜

There were middles of nights
when we weren't sure
where to go next,
only that we had to go somewhere.
You would rest your head on my chest,
sink into it, I let your hand wander
under the covers, so familiar
it was like it was my own.

Something we could not let go:
        all the time spent, the conversations
    run and rerun, we didn't think we would
have the strength to have them
        with another person.
We would wake, dizzy,
reeling from the heat of an accidental night
    spent together, the inertia
of being one unit,
no energy left to pull
        ourselves apart.

                    ⌁

Think of the biggest, smallest
thing you know: the whale's tough hide,
kelp clearing a path. That blue giant
from so far down it's as if it was spawned
from the core of the earth; too frightening
to imagine anything bigger—
its parents, or its creator.

Surely the movement of the earth
from far away is like a piano underwater,
pianissimo, water talking to itself.

                    ⌁

All of this talk is just talk.
The truth is, we will never know
our own future, not even
our own past.

       ~

If Sagan and his crew really wanted an alien,
you say, they would look to the octopus.
With its tangle of fingers, its mysterious
upside-down underworld,
like something you'd see
in a movie.

       ~

The girl on the beach
wants to know where
we will be in ten years.

Will we believe in God then,
or in something bigger than
God, like American currency

or a cure for loneliness?

       ~

A sigh.

You tell me I'm afraid all this probing
will have been a waste.
That we are walking with a flashlight
down empty halls.

~

What about the girl!

Our memories may be scrap
to the girl on the beach,
but is it a waste
that I got to dream her?

     I know: in your dream,
     the girl wades into the water
     in search of something unspecified,
     something to please her.

Aerial

Sunday Night After the Snowstorm

The world shuts down.
Twice in one hour, I get my mother's car
stuck in the grooves on your street; men from surrounding
houses rush out to help me push.

What do we do? We walk to a second-run cinema
down the road from your house.
Our steps are heavy and awkward.
We're like men on the moon.

The movie begins: it's something gruesome
in which children are hurt,
but the theatre is warm. Then, suddenly,
a black mark on the screen
moves, flies up, swoops down—

a bat hangs over our heads
like a bad idea. In the dusty
projection-light, we can see its delicate
wings, its body that is all
elbows. We try to watch the screen,
but are distracted by movement,
by distance and depth,

by something so small and intricate
we can't help but wonder where on earth
it came from.

Sentient

a.

Later in the photos
we see shapes. The smoky masses
of shadow near us, and beyond.

We have no proof now: the goats blurred
into brown spots, the elk
into faint furry smudges—of paint, maybe,
they could be anything. But we know

what we saw: smears and stains
of all kinds—antlers, hooves,

a corner of wing, a flash of tail.
Two prints and four: at the motel
in Wawa they led right
up to our door.

b.

Later in the photos
we can't tell which way's back
and which forward. Too much
glare. In the photos, there's no centre,

no point of origin; like looking for the lines
between prairie and everything else,

like looking for an island on land.
In the stretched highway panoramas,
there's no telling dawn from twilight,
near from far, no defining
how we gained an hour
three times, no watches
or stopped town clocks, no way

to piece together story from such
casual, indifferent remains. Listen—

you are concerned about time
and space and how
you'd look from above.
Dotted lines are in your head.

Thirty Years Ago Today

My childless mother and father
cruise-control down Highway 401
towards home. They make their usual
stop at Grier's, for coffee
and sandwiches. The place is
empty, abandoned even
of employees.

This is how I see the restaurant:
oversize Fifties decor—
despite the year, 1969—
the tables and chairs silver
and red plastic; the counter
an elongated ellipse;
mini jukeboxes
at every table like the consoles
of a giant machine, and the doors
to the kitchen have those
head-size windows like portholes
to the sea or sky.

After a wait, a man looks out.
"We were watching TV.
They landed, it's a miracle."
He invites them to the back
to watch the footage.

The cook makes them lunch,
his eyes distracted by
the staticky screen:

through metallic snow
the outlines of men
give the finger-sign O.K.

Back in the car, she talks
fast: what this means,
what will happen next.
He stares at the road ahead
with tears at the corners

of his eyes, and they drive
a road so slightly
curved it seems flat.

Road Movie

This landscape is shameless in its heavy-
handed portrayal of wasted beauty:
the grain elevator, cattle, the wavy
sky, its white heart beating cruel and mute.
The director went on about himself
for far too long: so much could have been cut—
reels upon reels of stock footage on shelves,
gathering dust like educational films that bored us. But
extra verses of anthems we never sing
stay fixed in our heads—famine and ruin
mark the highway, our spirit etched in yellow grass.

Convinced I've not forgotten anything
I think of the air surrounding you (in
this car smelling of oranges and gas).

Nights Above Fraser Street

Police car cruises a slow patrol. Same one
three times. Long-legged women dressed
in silver and black, hair pulled back tight,
are hard as rock and bone, shivering.
Number 8 bus sparks and sizzles
casting fat shadows on a short man
carrying a baseball bat like an umbrella.
One way, there are yellow lights like
forest eyes, reflected in thick black water.
The other way slopes up and up,
lit by white lampfog and video store neon.

The woman next door leans out her open window
wearing a hat and gloves; her copper-tipped
cigarette draws loops in the air in front of her.
She has never noticed me. She spells out
her name, her address, tomorrow's
to-do list, with her fire and smoke.
She tips ash ceremoniously into a coffee can.
Language, like fire, is a discovery—
not an invention. Night upon night, the woman sits
and lets particles of dust, words, spill
through the open frame of my glass,
and in this way, we talk.

The Bid

four diamonds
means never saying sorry, never having to say
anything. insurance against loneliness, debt, bad karma,
teenage boys who want to help you to your car so they
can rifle through your pockets and your purse, at least they would
if you weren't smarter. the din of the street is deafening.
you wish for the clip-clop of a different time—this era's ending
and you feel sorry no one seems to know what it means,
that no one is mourning.

three spades
means stop right there, hold your hands up
high so they can feel you all over. means rainy
days and mondays and your own private
declaration of war on the government, cops,
on street vendors and the last of the
dyed-in-the-wool hardhat-wearers. architects
are ruining my life, you think, as you shield
your eyes and cross the street.

two clubs
means strange coincidences happen
wherever you go: eddie in the smoke shop
finds a winning 6/49 as he's mopping; carla has just
been reunited with her long-lost identical twin.
she thought she was dead, but there's order
to the world and you are held safe and still
against its beating chest as it spins and spins and you swallow
another tab, thinking it can only get better, and it does.

one heart
means there's no room for gambling, this is it,
there is only membrane between you and everyone else,
and how easily will that tissue be tested, teased,
torn? we'll barely feel it. it will happen on a grey day
when everyone's stepping over swollen earthworms: someone
will fall in love, and the rest of us will feel a slow
contraction, something sticky stretched and gone, a contract
forever X'd on invisible lines between us.

His Version

He, too, abandoned his lessons early.
He had known some things,
had been tinkering. It began
like the cat tiptoeing along
the keys, the satisfaction of random
notes: plink, pleedle pleedle,
cling clang clung.
Which progressed to chords
that sounded right,
like something prehistoric
he had unearthed.
He was creating the clips
and murmurs of a music
that pours itself all over you.

But then he was sat down.
Taught to bend some parts
and hold others still,
to play the scales:
sliding, smooth,
shale shining under sand,
a tough protective skin.

And on to "The Birch Canoe,"
and "Little Brown Jug." *But,* he
says now, *I wanted to
make "Little Brown Jug"
swing.* He bent, wavered
where he pleased. Rules
not followed; lessons
called off. The piano
unplayed, a tent left
standing in the desert.

Years later, it is enough
to finger an organ
with headphones on—
outside, the dull rolling of fingers on keys.
But inside those soft conches
he can hear time's rustle,
bags of polished teeth and bones,
and piece by piece,
he begins to assemble.

Thinning

Michael is cleaning out the weeds
on the front lawn; I'm shocked
by how many of them I mistook
for flowers. My landlord's feeling
good these days, anxious
to clean house while he's up
to it. Less excited about going
back to work at the funeral home.
He wears a falling-apart T-shirt,
sweats, tears at the unaccountable
weeds in the yard, yanking
with his whole body. Pulling up
moisture-suckers, attachments, roots,
he tells me about his friend, also
with HIV, who sits about all day,
feeling, well—sorry.
The friend, he believes, is
one of those. Michael leans
with all his weight, loosening
the rope-like vines that have
nowhere else to go,
that have entered the earth
and will not leave.

Autumn Detail

The paint on the house next door is still
drying. Burnt Sienna coming to a gold-
red, the outside of the house
like the gut of salmon.

Insides on the outside: blood
so personal I hate to see it, but love
the raw smell like wet stones.
The unplanned. The shine
of every transitional moment,
of every detail first obscured, then clear.

Every time I leave the house
I see what's changing—the false
pink of fading synagogue walls,
trees discarding their loveliest parts.
We are in the process

of turning nothing around into
something, of rolling everything
over messily to see what's
underneath, what's next
to the earth, and here
we are: on the underside, two
slick, wet passengers, growing
on one another.

When You Clean the Aquarium

you lean over with your back,
instead of bending
at your knees. You try to get in
the corners, but often give up.

In the four months we've been living
together, you've cleaned the tank
three times. Concentration
buckles you.

You go to the kitchen sink to dump
the dirty water from the bucket, ask me
to keep an eye on the betta, Mingus,
make sure he doesn't jump out,

try to make a swim for it,
his fuchsia tail feathering him over the edge,
swimming turned flight—
fish alchemy.

Would the flutter of his caudal fin
be the same as in water? Snapping out anger, the all-at-once whip
that works so well diving beneath a ceramic house?
Will he know how to fly when he hits the air?
            (Repeating his mantra: *Breathe, man, breathe!*)

The fresh water you pour into the aquarium
clouds up, but I can't help noticing the light
coming through, and the calm—your temperate voice
as you reassure him, as you tell him to stay put.

Aerial

You are a thief again—
a little boy stuffing toys
into his corduroy pants at Zellers.
You didn't get caught, but
the guilt drove you to bury
them, unopened, in the backyard.
Part of you thought an enormous tree
full of toys might bloom. You laugh,
can't imagine yourself small
and paralysed with fear, with wonder.

I can see it, though—
just as I can see you with your string
of brunettes, the new one with a tattoo
on her inner thigh:
the Chinese character
of another man's name.

I wonder if other people
can see us as we are—
me, sunburned, sideways on a towel,
pretending to read a magazine,
sometimes brushing your foot with mine.
You on holiday, reading a book
about what matters in the universe,
asking what to do
when you're between a woman's legs,
how to read that universe, what
the order is.

You, the planet—
meaning *wanderer*, wanting to hover close,
to orbit her white moons,
you, the explorer,
who can't help wanting to plant
things, to see what grows.

Acknowledgements

Some of the poems in this collection appeared in *The Antigonish Review, Contemporary Verse 2, Descant, Event, The Fiddlehead, Grain, The Malahat Review, Pottersfield Portfolio, Prairie Fire, The Seattle Review*, as well as in the anthologies *Vintage 2000* (Ronsdale Press) and *Larger than Life: An Anthology of Celebrity* (Black Moss Press). My sincere thanks to the editors of those publications.

In 2003, "The Octopus" (published in *PRISM international*, 41:1) was a finalist for a National Magazine Award. My thanks to the National Magazine Awards Foundation and *PRISM* editor Billeh Nickerson.

The epigraph for the poem "Trajectory" comes from the poem "Prelude" by Tomas Tranströmer, translated by Robin Fulton, in *Selected Poems 1954-1986*, HarperCollins.

And thank you to:

The institutions that supported the writing of these poems: Canada Council for the Arts, Banff Writing Studio, B.C. Festival of the Arts, and UBC's Creative Writing Department.

The many mentoring poets who contributed to the poems in this collection (or earlier versions of them): Richard Sanger, Tom Wayman, George McWhirter, Keith Maillard, Don McKay, A. F. Moritz, Sharon Thesen, Ross Leckie, and Kate Braid.

My editor, John Barton, for his care.

The poet friends who gave the gift of brilliant feedback on the poems in this book. In particular, Marita Dachsel, Jeff Morris, and Laisha Rosnau. Also, Nancy Lee, Pam Galloway, Fiona Tinwei Lam, and Aurian Haller.

My family, for their incredible support and (sometimes unwitting) inspiration, including: my mother, Judy Harper; my brother, Benjamin Harper, and Catherine Bermingham; my uncle, Wayne Edmonds; my sister-cousin, Dawn Edmonds; all my family in Brampton, Toronto, Barrie, California, and North Bay; and my father, Peter Harper.

The friends and surrogate families who have been tirelessly encouraging over the years, and who will occasionally see themselves in these poems. In Ontario: Colin Campbell (without whom "The Octopus" wouldn't exist), Krista Black, Cheryl Boisclair, Elizabeth Skinner, Tara DiDomizio, Geoff Lee, Dave Eadie, Frank Kocis, Chris Reiss, and Dan Fisher. In B.C.: Steve Galloway, Charlotte Gill, Heather Frechette, the Golden Brads, the Ad Lib gals, the kindred spirits at VFS, and Susan, Rodger, and Brad Morris.

Finally, thank you again to Jeff Morris, the other passenger.